A New True Book

ARCHAEOLOGY

By Dennis B. Fradin

This "true book" was prepared
under the direction of
Illa Podendorf,
formerly with the Laboratory School,
University of Chicago

 CHILDRENS PRESS, CHICAGO

American Indian pipe with bear

For my sister, Lori Fradin

PHOTO CREDITS

Hillstrom Stock Photos—©Jack Lund, 11

Jerry Hennen—2, 25

Root Resources—©Loren M. Root, Cover
                  ©Mary Root, 22 (bottom)
                  ©Jean M. Grant, 35
                  ©L. Stepal, 33

Lorraine Matys—4 (bottom left)

Reinhard Brucker—4 (top), 8, 19, 42, 43 (right), 45 (right)

Mark Rosenthal—22 (top)

Melaine Ristich—4 (bottom right)

Jeff Rotman—34

Allan Roberts—6 (right), 41

James M. Mejuto—9 (2 photos), 31, 39, 43 (left), 45 (left)

Sharon Hatch—14 (2 photos), 37

Historical Pictures Service, Chicago—12, 17, 21 (2 photos), 27 (3 photos), 29, cover

Virginia Grimes—6 (left), 21 (top right)

COVER—Uncovering Indian skeleton,
Hacker Site, Illinois

Library of Congress Cataloging in Publication Data

Fradin, Dennis B.
  Archaeology.

  (A New true book)
  Includes index.
  Summary: Briefly discusses the techniques and tools archaeologists use to locate and study artifacts from the past and highlights milestones in the history of archaeology.
    1. Archaeology—Juvenile literature. [1. Archaeology]
I. Title.
CC171.F7 1983   930.1   83-7309
ISBN 0-516-01691-1   AACR2

TABLE OF CONTENTS

Above: Egyptian mummies and coffins
Right: Roman statue from 3rd century
in Rhodes, Greece
Below: Sphinx in Egypt

WHAT IS ARCHAEOLOGY?

Did you ever see an Egyptian mummy in a museum? Or statues dug from ancient cities? If so, you already have been introduced to archaeology.

Archaeology is a science. It is the study of very old objects such as buildings, bones, and tools.

Above: Archaeologists use a sifting
screen to examine Roman ruins
found along Hadrian's Wall in England.
Right: Arrowheads

The scientists who find
and study old objects are
called archaeologists. They
look for objects that are
many hundreds or
thousands of years old.
They study old objects to
learn how people lived in
ancient times.

SECRETS IN THE EARTH AND SEA

More than a million years ago the first people appeared on earth. As time passed, people learned to make fire and tools. They began to grow crops. They built villages and then cities.

History has been written in books for only a few hundred years. How can we learn about people who

Egyptian tomb

lived before the writing of books? The best way is to study the things they left behind: tools, jewelry, statues, houses, ships, coins, and tombs.

Many old objects have been covered by thousands

Above: News bulletin written in hieroglyphics more than 3,200 years ago during the reign of King Amenhotep.
Left: Stemmed cup from Mycenae, an ancient civilization that flourished on the Greek mainland from 1400 to 1200 B.C.

of years of dirt. Others
lie deep beneath the sea.
Archaeologists try to figure
out where ancient relics
are located. Then they
dig through the ground—
or dive into the ocean—
in search of them.

A SHORT HISTORY OF ARCHAEOLOGY

Up until the 1700s, people had little interest in studying things from the past. When they found ancient objects (called artifacts), they kept the ones made of gold. Less valuable ones were often thrown away!

In 1748 a farmer digging in a field in Italy struck an underground wall. A digging crew then unearthed

Forum, or marketplace, at Pompeii as it appears after excavation

an ancient city. It was
Pompeii, which had been
destroyed by a volcano
nearly 1,700 years earlier.
The excavation (digging)
at Pompeii was one of the
first done in an organized
way.

11

Covered by volcanic lava and ash, these bodies have been preserved since A.D. 63.

But archaeologists of the 1700s still mainly sought treasure. They tossed aside many other artifacts in search of it.

Sir Flinders Petrie (1853-1942) was one of the first archaeologists to study everything he found. Petrie worked in Egypt during the late 1800s. When Petrie dug, he searched the earth "inch by inch," as he described it. Petrie found pottery, tools, and other items used by Egyptians in their daily life. Because he worked so carefully, Petrie is called the "Father of Modern Archaeology."

Today's archaeologists use the "inch by inch" method. They keep detailed

Today archaeologists carefully record their findings at a dig. They take photographs and draw maps to scale showing exactly how artifacts were positioned when they were uncovered.

records of everything they find. They know that the smallest artifact can help us understand how ancient people lived.

FAMOUS DISCOVERIES

As a boy, Heinrich Schliemann (1822-1890) liked stories about ancient Greece. He loved the *Iliad*, a story by the Greek poet Homer. It tells of the war between the Greeks and the people of Troy. No one knew where Troy had been located. Schliemann decided that one day he'd find this lost city.

When Schliemann was forty-two, he began his search for Troy. Schliemann studied the *Iliad.* He decided that the city was located near the Aegean Sea in what is now Turkey. He went there and began to dig.

Ruins at Troy. Archaeologists have found the remains of nine cities. Each new city was built on the same site after the previous city was destroyed.

In the early 1870s Schliemann found the ruins of Troy. It was one of nine cities built on top of each other.

Another big find occurred in 1799. That year a French soldier found a stone tablet in Egypt. On the stone was ancient Egyptian writing called hieroglyphics. Because the tablet was found near the village of Rosetta, it was called the Rosetta Stone.

The message in hieroglyphics was also written in Greek.

Rosetta Stone carried the same message in Egyptian hieroglyphics (picture signs), Egyptian demotic writing (shorter form of writing), and in Greek, an ancient but well-known language. Because of this find, later archaeologists learned how to read Egyptian writing.

The French archaeologist Jean Francois Champollion (1790-1832) studied the tablet. First he translated the Greek. From that he figured out the hieroglyphics.

In the early 1900s Howard Carter (1873-1939) searched for an ancient tomb in Egypt. In 1922 he found it. In the tomb were many items belonging to Tutankhamen, a king who lived more than 3,300 years ago. Carter also found the mummy of "King Tut."

Howard Carter (below) and a worker examine the second of
a series of coffins that protected the mummy of King Tutankhamen.
Entrance to the tomb of "King Tut" at Luxor (above).

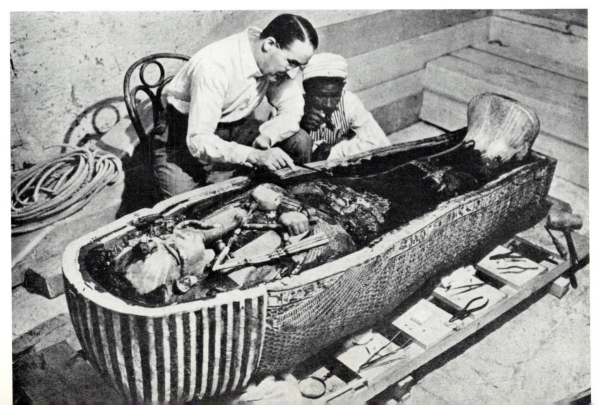

Chichén Itzá, a Mayan temple

Indian mounds in Georgia

Important finds have been made in the Americas, too. Hundreds of years ago, the Americas were home to many groups of Indians. The Mayas lived in Central America. The Incas lived in South America. The Aztecs lived in Mexico. Indians called Mound Builders lived in what is now the United States.

John Lloyd Stephens (1805-1852) was one of the first to explore Central America's Mayan ruins. The Maya were an advanced people who built cities, studied astronomy, and had a written language. Many Mayan buildings have been uncovered in the past century.

Thomas Jefferson (1743-1826), the third president of the United States, was also an

Archaeologists uncover bones in an Indian burial mound.

amateur archaeologist. He
was one of the first to
explore an Indian mound.
Since Jefferson's time, many
Indian mounds have been
explored in the United States.

25

DISCOVERIES BY CHILDREN

Children have made important finds, too.

In 1879 a man and his nine-year-old daughter, Maria, entered a cave at Altamira, Spain.

The two had often explored this cave near their castle.

As her father dug for tools and bones, Maria became bored. She took a candle and went to a

Examples of prehistoric
cave paintings found in
Altamira, Spain
(top and bottom left) and
Lascaux, France (above).

corner of the cave. Looking
up at the ceiling, Maria
saw paintings of animals.
The cave paintings—made

more than twelve thousand
years ago—are among the
oldest art works ever
discovered.

In the summer of 1947
a shepherd boy,
Mohammed Adh-Dhib, was
tending goats in Palestine.
One got lost. Mohammed
climbed a hill to find it.

On the hill Mohammed
spotted a cave. He
returned to the cave the
next day with a friend.
Inside, they found parts of

The Dead Sea Scrolls, found in an earthenware jar, are believed to be the oldest existing portions of the Bible. Here a religious leader holds a scroll that contains part of the Book of Isaiah.

the Bible written nearly two thousand years ago. Other parts of the Bible later were found nearby. Because they were found near the Dead Sea, these manuscripts are called the Dead Sea Scrolls.

KNOWING WHERE TO LOOK

The world is a big place. How do archaeologists know where to look for ancient relics? They don't just guess. Like detectives, they search for clues.

Old books often provide good clues. The Bible, the works of Homer, and other old manuscripts describe ancient towns. Some of

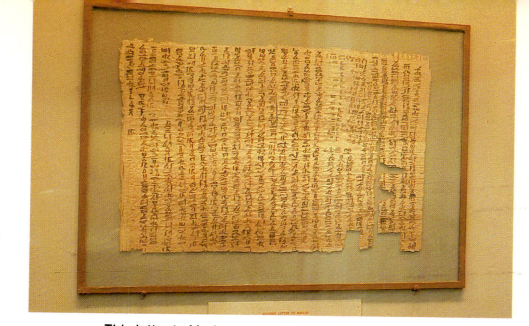

This letter to Merisu was written in August of the year 2002 B.C. In it the Egyptian author explains that conditions are bad and that the household is on rations. But no one should complain because "half a life is better than death." From such letters archaeologists can piece together life in the past.

those towns are still there—buried under layers of dirt. Archaeologists study the books to determine where the ancient sites may be located.

People often tell stories about past events. For example, people may tell of a sunken ship. Archaeologists listen to such stories for clues about the ship's location.

Archaeologists often use photographs taken from airplanes. They show things that can't be seen from the ground.

An aerial photo may show a piece of land to be more fertile than nearby

Ruins at Machu Picchu, an ancient Inca city on a mountain in Peru

land. This may be because ancient people worked the soil there.

Cameras are also used to spot undersea wrecks.

Diver investigates
a shipwreck
in the Red Sea.
Underwater cameras
can be used to find
sunken ships.

Archaeologists have many other tools to help them decide where to work. These include magnets, metal detectors, soil studies, and electrical tests of the ground.

Archaeologists pick up pieces of pottery used in 1800 B.C. in Elazig, Turkey.

DIGGING

It can take many
lifetimes to excavate a
site. Archaeologists have
been digging at Pompeii
since 1748. There's still
much to do there. Because

digging takes so long, archaeologists hate to waste time.

When they've found a likely site, they sink trial shafts. These are holes that show how far down the site goes. They also dig trial trenches. These show how long and wide the site is. Once they know the size of the site, archaeologists hire a crew and organize the digging.

Each object is examined carefully.

Pictures are taken of any object the crew finds. Then an archaeologist carefully removes the artifact from the ground with a little knife or brush.

37

HOW OLD IS IT?

Once archaeologists have found an artifact, they have several questions. A main one is: How old is it? Knowing the ages of artifacts helps chart the growth of civilization.

The archaeologist Christian Thomsen (1788-1865) worked out the Three Age System. The three are the Stone Age, Bronze Age, and Iron Age.

Display of Bronze Age objects

The Stone Age was
when people used stone
tools. It began over a
million years ago and
ended about five thousand
years ago. During the
Bronze Age people made
tools out of the metal

bronze. It extended from about five thousand years ago to around three thousand years ago. The Iron Age began about three thousand years ago. We are still in the Iron Age.

By learning what an artifact is made of, scientists obtain a very rough idea of its age. They also have ways to learn its age more exactly.

Skeleton of an Indian witch doctor

One important method is called carbon-14 dating. When living things die, they give off a substance called carbon 14. The longer an object has been dead, the less carbon 14 it has. By measuring the

41

Petrified wood has turned to stone.

amount of carbon 14 in a piece of wood or other object that once was alive, scientists can tell its age.

Carbon-14 dating only works for objects that lived within the past forty thousand years. Scientists have other methods to date objects older than that.

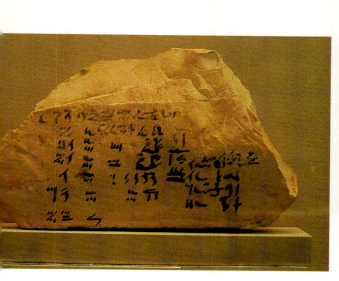

Examples of Egyptian hieroglyphics.
The stone (left) records payment
made to workers in 2000 B.C.

ALL KINDS OF ARCHAEOLOGISTS

There are other kinds of archaeologists besides those who dig for artifacts. Some translate old writing. Others work in museums.

43

Government archaeologists make sure that old sites aren't destroyed.

Many archaeologists teach. One good teacher can train hundreds of future archaeologists.

Many finds are yet to be made in archaeology. Sunken ships still lie underwater. Lost cities lie beneath the ground. Statues, caves, and mummies wait to

Above: Head found on an Egyptian
      sarcophagus (a limestone
      coffin).
Left: Tablet from 1415 B.C.
      dedicated to the Egyptian god Ra.

be found. Writing tablets
need to be translated.

   Perhaps you will become
an archaeologist. Then you
will help our human race
learn more about its past.

WORDS YOU SHOULD KNOW

A.D.—this refers to the years after the birth of Christ

aerial photographs(AIR•ee•il)—pictures taken from the air

amateur(AM•ah•cher)—one who does something without pay

ancient(AIN•chent)—very old

archaeologist(are•kay•OL•oh•gist)—a scientist who studies very old objects

archaeology(ar•kay•OL•uh•gee)—the scientific study of very old objects including buildings, bones, tools, and art works

artifacts(AR•tih•facts)—objects made by people of long ago

B.C.—this refers to the years before Christ was born

Bronze Age(BRAHNZ)—the period, starting about 5,000 years ago and ending about 3,000 years ago, when people made bronze tools

carbon-14 dating(CAR•bun)—a method to tell the age of old objects that were once alive

excavation(ex•kah•VAY•shun)—the process of digging

expedition(ex•ped•DIH•shun)—a trip made by a group for scientific study

fertile(FER•till)—good for plants to grow in

hierogylphics(hy•roh•GLIH•fix)—picture writing used by Egyptians, Aztecs, and several other peoples

Iron Age—the period, starting about 3,000 years ago and continuing to this day, when tools have been made of iron

magnets(MAG•netz)—objects that attract certain metals

manuscripts(MAN•yoo•scripts)—written or typed materials

metal detectors(MEH•til•dee•TEK•torz)—devices used to locate old coins and other metal objects

mound—a hill built by people

mummy(MUM•ee)—a dead body specially treated so that it will last for thousands of years

museum(myoo•zee•um)—a building where art works or historical materials are shown to the public

pick—a pointed instrument used for digging

relic —an object left from the past

Rosetta Stone(ro •ZET •ah) —an ancient tablet that helped scientists translate Egyptian hieroglyphics

site(SYTE) —location of something

Stone Age —the period, starting over a million years ago and ending about 5,000 years ago, when people made stone tools

Three Age System —a system in which human history is divided into the Stone, Bronze, and Iron ages

tomb(TOOM) —a place where a dead person is put

translate(TRANZ •late) —to convert the words of one language into the words of another language

trial shafts(TRYL SHAFTZ) —holes dug to find out how far down a site goes

trial trenches —cuts made in the ground to determine how far across a site extends

trowel(TROWL) —a little shovel used for digging

INDEX

About the Author

Dennis Fradin attended Northwestern University on a partial creative writing scholarship and graduated in 1967. He has published stories and articles in such places as Ingenue, The Saturday Evening Post, Scholastic, Chicago, Oui, *and* National Humane Review. *His previous books include the Young People's Stories of Our States series for Childrens Press and* Bad Luck Tony *for Prentice-Hall. He is married and the father of three children.*